I0475056

Develop Your Financial IQ

"Greatly Enhance Your Financial Sense In A Fun And Easy Way – And Take Control Of Your Finances Today!"

**from the library of the
New Thrive Learning Institute**

Published 2016 under Creative Commons License -
NonCommercial-ShareAlike 3.0 Unported

Get Related Materials

from Our Free Library

Instant Access – Join Here

Click or type into your browser:

http://livesensical.com/go/byob/

LEGAL NOTICE

The Publisher has striven to be as accurate and complete as possible in the creation of this report, notwithstanding the fact that he does not warrant or represent at any time that the contents within are accurate due to the rapidly changing nature of the Internet.

While all attempts have been made to verify information provided in this publication, the Publisher assumes no responsibility for errors, omissions, or contrary interpretation of the subject matter herein. Any perceived slights of specific persons, peoples, or organizations are unintentional.

In practical advice books, like anything else in life, there are no guarantees of income made. Readers are cautioned to reply on their own judgment about their individual circumstances to act accordingly.

This book is not intended for use as a source of legal, business, accounting or financial advice. All readers are advised to seek services of competent professionals in legal, business, accounting, and finance field.

Table of Contents

Chapter 1: Foundation in Financial IQ

Definition Of Insanity

Naturally, most if not all of us want and crave for something better. It is all part of us if we want a bigger car, a better house, buying good things for the family. We keep hoping for more but, in order to get what you don't have, you have got to do something you have never done before.

That simply means:

Doing the same thing over and over again YET expecting different results!

As an employee, you can't stay at the same job forever and hope that a miracle will happen and your boss will suddenly give you a raise. You will be lucky that there is no downsizing in your company. Switching to another company will only provide a short term solution to a long term problem.

Sure, you can take up a second or even third job, but do you have enough hours and stamina in a day to sustain it?

The bottom-line: Trading time for money isn't wise

financial sense in the long term. You keep on increasing the hours just to win the rat race, but in the end of the day, you are still a rat on the mill!

Increasing your wages only puts you in a higher tax bracket. Your salaries increase but so does your expenses on your house and car. How will you invest in yourself when all the time you spend working for a company, working for the government paying taxes and working for the bank paying off your house and car? What if you fall sick and can't work tomorrow? Will the government take care of your family?

I highly doubt so.

So isn't it time you take your finances a tad more seriously?

What Is Money?

You see, there are many ideas of what people think money is.

Some say it is a form of measurement.

Yes, but a measurement of what? Wealth? In the olden days, people measured wealth by how many cows, sheep and horses they had. But do people measure wealth today by your cows and horses? How about slaves? Was there a time where manpower is considered a hot commodity? Are slaves worth anything today? Are your dollar bills sitting in the bank going to protect you if a recession strikes the country? No, wealth can not be measured by the dollar bill.

Some say it is a form of power.

Yes, money can give you power, but if you are stuck on a desert island forever with a trillion dollars, will that money mean squat to you? If someone offered you water and a helicopter to fly out of there, you would trade all your money in a split second, so money is not an accurate measurement of power – it heavily depends on how and wisely you use it (hint!).

Many believe it is the root of all evil... and several others take on this belief without much questioning.

Now, now, now... money is NOT the root of all evil (otherwise, why do you think churches still accept monetary donation and charity?). The love of money is the root of all evil. Remember, money is an excellent servant but a terrible master. If you are trading your life away for the dollar, money then has power over your time and life.

And unless you have proper financial intelligence, the lack of money can spawn a lot of evil thinking and negative mindset as observed in primarily cheats, thieves, criminals, breakups, freeloaders, cheapskates, and more to name.

But what is money, really?

Money is an idea, backed by confidence.

While money has naturally been developed by merchants in the older days to replace the questionable barter system, money today is literally invented by the rich and wealthy.

Entrepreneurs are willing to part with their money to buy other people's time. Other people's time i.e. employees and self-employed people becomes their employer's asset and the employers this priceless resource to go on to create more wealth for themselves.

And here's the thing: as long as you work for money, you are enslaved by it! 80% - 90% of the populations today are being enslaved involuntarily.

What we don't realize is that there is a part of our soul

that cannot be bought at whatever price. Would you chop off your little finger if your boss offered you 24 months of your salary immediately? You and I know we are worth more than that. But when you hear of cases of people selling their body parts for cash in some countries, we can have our eyeballs pop out of our eye sockets.

On the other hand, we occasionally DO sell out a part of ourselves for money like a donkey and a carrot.

Awareness Before Change

Now don't get me wrong: I'm not banging on working at a job (I worked at one before I became an Internet Entrepreneur).

But let's face it: our needs today are growing more than ever before in any period of history. Prices go up, salaries don't. There are more baby boomers than ever and have very little pension to show for their decades of years of work efforts.

And there is no guessing to how many people really, really hate the unhealthy, hectic lifestyle of getting up early, coping with stress for most parts of the day, join traffic jams, spend more money and time in traveling, enjoy very little rest, and repeat the viscous cycle.

Definitely doesn't paint a nice financial and lifestyle picture, huh?

The first step to change is to be aware of the problem. Awareness before change (or ABC for short) is necessary if you are to make any changes in life to start taking control of your financial life and then get out of the rat race.

We need the awareness to know what state we are in so we know where we are going. For starters, indulge me in a quick exercise as we exit this chapter shortly:

Time And Money

There are generally 4 types of people in the world:

- No time, and no money.

Most employees fall into the category. You can't go shopping on a Tuesday afternoon or fire your boss whenever you like. Most employees can't even save money in their pension to last 3 years!

- No time, lots of money.

Self-employed, professionals and small business owners are in this category. They are slightly better off than the employee because they earn more, but they have to work even harder than employees to keep up with the diminishing profit margins, competition and servicing their customers.

- Got time, no money.

A lot of farmers, villagers, college dropouts or bums have lots of time but no money. Maybe ignorance is bliss, but without a stable source of income, how long can you last many days forward?

- Got time, and lots of money.

It is the category that big business owners, landlords, investors are in. Imagine, not having to work for money, but having money to work for you by investing them and earning profits by using your money to make money.

Short Quiz

1. Which one of the four categories are you currently in?

2. Which one category do you desire to be in tomorrow?

Chapter 2: Ways To Achieve Wealth

2 Wealth Building Models

Everyone wants to make more money, but people are generally split into two categories:

Those who bring results after they are promised wealth first

Or

Those who bring the results first, then are rewarded by others afterwards

Let's explore the two groups in depth.

Those who only move their butts after promised big fat paychecks are more like employees, freshmen, or mercenaries.

There is no right or no wrong with this kind of thinking, but consider: you are once again, trading your precious time for money. Instead of investing your time in an ASSET that generates money, you spend your time working on something that is short term, limited wealth, and does not give you income long after you have stopped working.

Consider also, that this kind of short term vision will only produce limited or temporary results at best. Ever seen a security guard asleep at work when the boss is not around?

Furthermore, the part where our emotions get the better of us is when we allow our lives to be run by chasing the dollar. It is evident whenever an employee is offered a higher salary, more medical benefits and longer vacations, that their heart starts pumping faster.

A higher salary doesn't mean less financial problems. On the contrary when your income goes up, your commitments, your tax bracket and your time spent in your company increases. The greater your salary, the weaker your position because if your boss is paying you a 5 figure income and calls for an emergency meeting, you had better rush over to the office even if you are halfway making love to your wife!

I think the best definition of an employee/boss relationship can be summed up as this.

An employee will only do the bare minimum to keep the boss from firing them and a boss will only pay the bare minimum to keep an employee from leaving.

Now let's explore the other group.

There are many creative people, inventors, entrepreneurs, and business leaders who fall into this category.

An entrepreneur is someone who always has good ideas.

The first obstacle we need to overcome if we want to succeed in the second group is to stop working for money. What does this mean? Isn't making money part and parcel of having good financial IQ?

What I mean by 'stop working for money' is not working for free. Rather, it means work so as to gain the necessary skills you need to be a successful entrepreneur (or inventor, investor). Allow me to illustrate:

If you lack the contacts for running a business, where would the best place be to look for contacts? Of course, your competitor's customers.

How about product knowledge? Then work with a company that will teach you all the ins and outs of the tricks of the trade.

Not familiar with the production line of a factory? Work

in one! Learn the ropes or manage the factory workers.

Fear of talking to people? Get a sales job where you will be forced to talk to lots of people. It is also a great way to develop perseverance!

Don't you know that the best education you can get is in real life! Not at a lecture hall.

The bottom-line is: not everybody has what it takes to succeed as an entrepreneur!

It is not that easy. Many lack the perseverance, the creative mindset, the financial capabilities or the necessary people to get the job done and usually give up too early before any results can be seen! The fastest way to get those skills to succeed is to learn them hands on and you even get paid in the process! Don't get absorbed with how much you are paid.

When Donald Trump was selecting candidates in The Apprentice, their first task was to go to the streets and sell lemonade! Many would find it a degrading task. But to The Donald, it was very important: If you can't even do something as simple as sell lemonade, how on earth can you handle a daunting task like running the Trump Empire?

Again, let me emphasize:

Would you trade time for short term money? (Money stops coming in when you stop)

Or

Trade time and money for a long term asset that generates you income? (Even long after you have stopped)

God created us with a brain. All we need to do is look around us and observe problems to overcome because every problem is an opportunity in disguise.

It is all up to you. You may or may not see the results in the short term, but by using our brains and the resources around us, we can create true value that others are willing to pay for what we have to offer.

3 Ways of Making Money

Let me summarize the 3 Ways of Making Money

- Trading Time For Money - employees, self-employed

- Manifesting & Using Creative Ideas - inventors, artists, programmers

- Leveraging on resources and other people - business people, leaders

If you are a professional, have you ever explored writing an e-book about your field of expertise? If well written, it could provide a new income stream, instead of you selling out your time serving your clients.

How about a computer programmer? You can come out with your own revolutionary product instead of selling your ideas to the company you work for.

How about real estate, instead of selling houses, you can pool financial sources to buy houses cheap, increase their value and sell them off at a higher price. It just takes a little time and research to find good ideas.

Is money a problem? Seek out loans if you can take the risk. Pool money from many investors or seek a grant. The sky is the limit when it comes to making money.

Again, which way do you want to achieve wealth? Answer: it's totally up to you

Chapter 3: The Most Important Rule in Investing

What Does Investing Mean To People?

What comes in to your mind when you mention the word investing?

Does it mean, putting your money in insurance, mutual funds, the stock market or even high-yield investments?

Other people might only think about investing when they are about to die and they haven't left anything for their offspring.

Some even shiver when they hear the word, often claiming that they have no money to invest or feel that is too complicated a subject to even discuss about.

Many people even invest heavily in health supplements, personal trainers and beauticians to make themselves live longer, healthier or even look younger! Imagine the advertising budget for beauty companies nowadays.

All these are legitimate concerns when it comes to investing, but I am talking about the most important investment a person can make in his lifetime.

Invest in Yourself

The most important and No.1 rule is "Invest in Yourself" – if you don't, who else will?

Your parents will only invest in your education only until you leave college. But that is just the basic necessities provided and does not teach you important lessons about financial education.

Would you depend on colleges or universities to teach you how to make money? Most colleges only teach you skills so you can earn money working for other people. How about business school? Honestly, if business lecturers are such experts at business, why are they still lecturing there instead of making a fortune in business ventures?

Would your boss teach you how to succeed in business so that one day, you will be in his position?

You and only you have to be proactive enough to take that responsibility

You see, when you invest in yourself, it means taking on the importance of educating yourself. Education not in the academic or technical sense, though they are necessary skills to be developed in life. Our education doesn't stop at college.

For most working adults, their education enters retardation stage after they leave college. They stop learning and therefore they stop growing. They only grow sideways from eating too much pizzas or take-out during their busy lunch breaks.

We know that IQ is important right? But why aren't the most intelligent people in the world the richest people in the world? There are many accountants and financial planners rushing to their cars every evening trying to beat the after work traffic congestions! They are not rich!

How about EQ or Emotional quotient? Do working hard, having a great attitude and a positive mindset solve our financial situation? These are important when running a business, but let me illustrate:

If you are driving from Boston to New York using the wrong road map, you won't get to our destination no matter how fast you drive your car (working hard)! You can work harder, but you would only get to the wrong destination faster! You may have the best attitude in the world or the most positive mindset, but you still won't get to New York (although the journey wouldn't bother you since you are feeling positive about it)

The Importance Of Financial Education

You must FIRST invest in your Financial IQ.

Having good financial IQ is not about saving tons of money or dumping them into mutual funds. It is developing a healthy relationship money and building a wealth of assets that will generate you money.

What does it take to develop your financial IQ?

Delayed gratification is one of the most important aspects to developing your financial IQ. Take this as a hypothetical example.

Would you pay for a pint of milk or a cow?

If you buy milk, it is consumed and it is over. You will have to buy milk over and over again when it is finished. Even if the milk costs less than a cow, in the long run, you will still be buying milk again and again.

Now, if a cow were to cost 50 times more than milk, you might pay through your nose when you purchase the cow, but after consuming 50 pints worth of milk from the cow, you would break even on your investment and save more money in the future. In fact, the cow might give birth to 2 or more calves and you could sell one of them for profit!

Get the idea?

EVERYONE is capable of creating wealth. When you take a beat up old car and give it an overhaul, paint it with a new coat of paint, and change a few more parts to make it start running again, you could sell that car for more money than if it was just a beat up old car. You would have created wealth in the process!

How about a farm? If you turn a farm into a country home getaway resort, wouldn't the value of the farm land increase manifold?

It is the same principle for chefs, computer programmers and craftsmen. The sum of the whole is greater than the parts. We are all capable of creating wealth even out of thin air and that is the first step to getting our creative juices flowing.

The value of anything is defined by supply and demand.

You don't need to be a Major in economics to

understand this. Money is just an idea. Remember the desert island example? The true measurement of money is not the cents or dollars it represents.

If you have developed a product that people want, would they pay more to you than usual? Would you apply your skills in creating good assets?

Bottom-line is this:

Invest in assets that bring long term value. Anything that brings you more income is an asset. Don't invest too much in liabilities like cars or boats.

Even houses are not considered assets until they are fully paid off (If you lost your job tomorrow and you can't pay for your house, is your house an asset or liability?)

Are you willing to step out of your comfort zone and pay the price for financial IQ or ignore the signs of the times and expect your boss, the government and the bank to take care of you financially for the rest of your life, living below your means and never taking risks to better your family's future?

Chapter 4: How To Get Out Of A Financial Mess

There are two methods I can recommend about getting out of a financial mess.

Defensive Strategies

The first one is defensive:

Cut down what you are already spending on. You can't start a business being in a financial mess. Cash Flow is more important than revenue. And you need to have lots of cash flow coming from your pockets if you are going to succeed.

Here are some things you can cut down on

- Smoking – if you can't quit, just cut down on a few sticks

- Alcohol – booze can drain your finances faster than a running tap

- Night outs – spend some nights at home thinking about making more money

- Gambling – if you plan to gamble, it is better to gamble in a business

- Vacation and Country Clubs – you won't die without a few memberships
- Food – eat healthily and you can even think clearer
- Laziness – The biggest thing that will hold you back!

Most important of all, don't buy anything that constitutes a liability. A liability is anything that takes money out of your pocket no matter what they are worth in the future. Think in terms of cash flow. What can I invest in today that will give me funds tomorrow?

Now let's move on to offensive strategies:

Offensive Strategies

One of the best, low-cost ways to invest in your business skills is to join a Network Marketing company. There are many other options such as starting a traditional business or maybe even an Online Business.

But if you want to guarantee yourself something concrete where business skills are concern, my take is on Network Marketing.

Regardless of what you have heard about this industry or how much money people have lost there, the biggest reason why I would recommend everyone to invest in a network marketing company is because of what you can learn there, and not because of how much money you can make (although it would be fantastic if you can make a living out of it).

You see, network marketing companies are the one place where people will share their trade secrets FREELY. It is logical because in order for your upline to succeed, they will want you to succeed as well! Therefore, they will not hold back in teaching you the skills of a business person.

Furthermore, the relatively low cost of investing in a network marketing company will amaze you for what you can learn for the price you are paying (a few bottles of vitamins and a business kit for the experience of a lifetime!) They will patiently train you in the attitudes and business skills you need to succeed in this industry.

Basically, you can't succeed in network marketing with an employee's mindset. A network marketing company will train you in sales, communication, teamwork, leadership, positive thinking, self-improvement, time and money investment as well as the support of your upline as a personal coach and mentor. I dare say that even if you didn't make a cent, but diligently went through their program, the skills you develop will last a lifetime.

You can also develop skills by attaching yourself to an insurance agency. The job may be challenging, but those companies will also teach you the same skills above and maybe even gain a few tips on financial planning as well.

How about an Internet business? If you have the aptitude for computers, Internet businesses offer a low cost, high-profit margin business that can earn a lot of money and tap into a worldwide market.

Other places you can learn about business skills can be found at financial planning courses, real estate investment courses, time management courses and lots more.

All these I have suggested will be the safest way you can start a new business. You are only spending a few hundred to a thousand dollars in start-up and education. A traditional business might be too risky for someone without any business experience. You invest tens of thousands of dollars and you might struggle trying to break even. But once you have developed the skills above, you will have a higher chance of succeeding.

The most important thing of all besides a good learning attitude are the people you mix around with.

It has been said before; you are the sum of the five people you spend the most time with!

This is very hard to swallow but imagine if you start talking to your five beer drinking, poker buddies that you want to go out on your own and make a fortune, what would they tell you? They would laugh their socks off before tearing your ego into a million pieces!

At the heart of man lies jealousy. They don't want to see the people around them succeed. If you succeed, it makes them look bad. They know in their hearts that they are going no where yet they embrace that lifestyle and pull you down with them. They will steal your dream, and rob you of your financial freedom if you are not careful!

The key point to remember is: Only mix with Positive thinking people!

Positive thinking is not wishful thinking. A wishful thinker is a dreamer who doesn't take action. Positive thinking is backed by action and you will feel the energy of people who believe in you and support your dreams.

If you hang out with ducks, you will quack... but if you hang out with eagles, you will soar!

So start looking for people who will follow your vision or are willing to grow together with you.

Lastly, you must BELIEVE IN YOURSELF!

The task of stepping out of your comfort zone may seem terrifying and many will not support your dream. They may even go on the offensive even if you don't share your dream. That person may even be your parents or your spouse.

Then you will be faced with the question, is my financial freedom worth the price I am paying now? Can I live another day with the same routine, the same job, the same paycheck or the same drudgery? If the answer is no, then take action NOW. Not tomorrow, you will wake up and forget about your dream.

Write down your desire on a piece of paper and hang on tight to it everyday. Share it with someone positive and take that first step.

You won't regret it.

To Your Financial Freedom!

Bonus

Get Related Materials

from Our Free Library

Instant Access – Join Here

Click or type into your browser:

http://livesensical.com/go/byob/

www.ingramcontent.com/pod-product-compliance
Lightning Source LLC
Chambersburg PA
CBHW021856170526
45157CB00006B/2474